MAXIMUM SPEED

CRAZY
CARS

Rob Colson

Published in 2023 by Enslow Publishing, LLC
29 East 21st Street, New York, NY 10010

Copyright © 2021 Wayland, an imprint of Hachette Children's Group

Series editor: John Hort
Designer: Ben Ruocco
Produced by Tall Tree Ltd

All rights reserved. No part of this book may be reproduced
in any form without permission in writing from the publisher, except by a reviewer.

Manufactured in the United States of America

CPSIA compliance information: Batch #CSENS23: For further information contact
Enslow Publishing LLC, New York, New York at 1-800-398-2504.

Please visit our website, www.enslowpublishing.com. For a free color catalog of all our high-quality books,
call toll free 1-800-398-2504 or fax 1-877-980-4454.

Cataloging-in-Publication Data

Names: Colson, Rob.
Title: Crazy cars / Rob Colson.
Description: New York : Enslow Publishing, 2023. | Series: Maximum speed | Includes glossary and index.
Identifiers: ISBN 9781978531024 (pbk.) | ISBN 9781978531048 (library bound) | ISBN 9781978531031 (6pack) | ISBN 9781978531055 (ebook)
Subjects: LCSH: Automobiles--Juvenile literature.
Classification: LCC TL147.C66 2023 | DDC 629.222--dc23

Picture credits:

FC-front cover, BC-back cover, t-top, b-bottom, l-left, r-right, c-centre

FC dimcars/Shutterstock.com, FC jamesteohart/Shutterstock.com, BC Phillip Rubino/Shutterstock.com, 1 Frolthy/Shutterstock.com, 5t Nick Lazarnick, 5br Opel, 6 Christopher Halloran/Shutterstock.com, 8tl Paul Hermans/Creative Commons, 8bl Nimbus227, 8br Library of Congress, 9t Iain Cochrane/Shutterstock.com, 9b Heritage Image Partnership Ltd/Alamy Stock Photo, 10tl Andrew Bone/Creative Commons, 10bl Joe deSouza, 10-11 General Motors, 11br Colin Furze, 12tl Daderot, 12b Insomnia Cured Here, 12-13, 13t Bri ham, 13cr National Motor Museum/Heritage Images/Getty Images, 14bl jwbruijn, 14r action sports/shutterstock.com, 15t National Library of France, 15b Photo Works/Shutterstock.com, 16tl Andrew Harker/Shutterstock.com, 16–17 David Madison/Contributor/Getty Images, 16bl Shutterstock.com, 17t Fouad A. Saad/Shutterstock.com, 17b Shutterstock.com, 18–19, 19tl Aussieinvader.com, 19tr, 19cr Jules1982/Creative Commons, 20tr Juerg Schreiter/Shutterstock.com, 20–21 NHRA, 21t Gunter Nezhoda/Shutterstock.com, 21b twm1340/Creative Commons, 22l Maserati Spa, 22–23, 23t Daimler AG, 23br Oskar Schuler/Shutterstock.com, 24–25, 25b Frolphy/Shutterstock.com, 24b Toyota, 26ct Mr.choppers/Creative Commons, 26cb Koenigsegg, 26–27 Max Earey/Shutterstock.com, 27tl Automobili Lamborghini S.p.A., 27tr Rimac, 28–29 Nuon Hans-Peter van Velthoven/Creative Commons, 29t Jason Benz Bennee/Shutterstock.com, 29c Sunswift/University of New South Wales

Find us on

CONTENTS

- SPEED ON FOUR WHEELS — 4
- OFFICIAL SPEED RECORDS — 6
- THE BLUE BIRDS — 8
- JET CARS — 10
- SPEED IN THE SIXTIES — 12
- PIONEERING WOMEN — 14
- BREAKING THE SOUND BARRIER — 16
- SPEED OF THE FUTURE — 18
- TOP FUEL DRAGSTERS — 20
- TRACK RACING FORMULA 1 — 22
- SPEED AND ENDURANCE — 24
- FASTEST CARS ON THE ROAD — 26
- POWERED BY THE SUN — 28
- GLOSSARY — 30
- SPEED FILE — 31
- INDEX — 32

SPEED ON FOUR WHEELS

Since they were invented, cars have been pushed to maximum speed, whether on the road or on a race track. The land speed record is the highest speed reached by a car. The record has been broken by many different kinds of car, including electric cars, steam-powered cars, and rocket cars.

ELECTRIC BATTLE

The first official land speed record was set in 1898 by French driver Gaston Chasseloup-Laubat. Behind the wheel of an electric Jeantaud car, he completed a 0.6-mile (1-km) course in 57 seconds, giving an average speed of 39 miles (63 km) per hour. Over the next year, Chasseloup-Laubat battled for the record with Belgian Camille Jenatzy. Also driving an electric car, Jenatzy became the first person to break the 62-mile (100-km) per hour barrier in 1899, setting a record that would last three years.

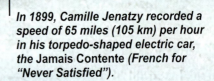

In 1899, Camille Jenatzy recorded a speed of 65 miles (105 km) per hour in his torpedo-shaped electric car, the *Jamais Contente* (French for "Never Satisfied").

EARLY SPEED

1899
Camille Jenatzy
Jamais Contente, electric motor | 65 miles (105 km) per hour

1898
Gaston Chasseloup-Laubat
Jeantaud, electric motor | 39 miles (63 km) per hour

⬆ FROM STEAM TO ROCKETS

In 1902, the speed record was taken by a car powered by a steam engine. Frenchman Leon Serpollet reached 75 miles (120 km) per hour in his oval-shaped car, nicknamed the *Easter Egg*. In 1906, American Fred Marriott took the record, reaching 128 miles (206 km) per hour in his *Stanley Steamer* (above). This set a record for any steam-powered vehicle, which stood for more than 100 years. From 1922 to 1963, the land speed record was held by cars powered by gas engines. Since then, **rocket-powered cars** have taken over.

The first rocket car to be built was called the Opel-Rak. It was made in the 1920s by German manufacturer Fritz von Opel.

1906
Fred Marriott
Stanley Steamer, steam engine | 128 miles (206 km) per hour

1902
Leon Serpollet
Easter Egg, steam engine | 75 miles (120 km) per hour

1922
Kenelm Guinness
Sunbeam 350 hp, gas engine | 134 miles (215 km) per hour

OFFICIAL SPEED
RECORDS

The first organization to officially record land speed records was the Automobile Club of France in 1902. Since 1924, record attempts have been standardized and follow rules set down by the FIA (International Federation of Automobiles).

THE RULES
All attempts at the land speed record must follow the FIA's rules to gain official recognition. The speed is recorded as the average of two runs of a fixed length on the same course in opposite directions. This means that cars cannot take advantage of winds or set a record by driving downhill.

In addition to world record attempts, every August Bonneville hosts a "Speed Week" during which hundreds of racing enthusiasts test out their machines.

FLAT COURSES
To reach maximum speed in both directions, drivers need a course that is as flat as possible. Up to 1935, courses were generally marked out on beaches. But since 1935, record attempts have been made on desert courses, such as the Bonneville Salt Flats in Utah, USA.

RECORDS IN WHEEL-DRIVEN CARS

1926
JG Parry-Thomas
Babs | 170 miles (274 km) per hour

❯ FLYING START

The FIA regulates a range of different records, but the most prestigious is the Outright World Land Speed Record. The cars are given a flying start, meaning that they are allowed to reach full speed before they pass the starting line of the course, which is normally 1 mile (1.6 km) long.

⌄ DANGER ON THE SANDS

In the 1920s, many record attempts were made on Pendine Sands beach in Wales. Today, vintage cars race one another on the beach every year for fun. However, breaking speed records is also very dangerous, and many drivers have lost their lives. The first to die was Welsh driver JG Parry-Thomas (right), who lost control of his car, *Babs*, when attempting the record on Pendine Sands in 1927.

1932
Malcolm Campbell
Campbell-Napier-Railton Blue Bird | 254 miles (409 km) per hour

1947
John Cobb
Railton Mobil Special | 394 miles (634 km) per hour

1964
Donald Campbell
Bluebird CN7 | 403 miles (649 km) per hour

THE BLUE BIRDS

Between the 1920s and the 1960s, Briton Malcolm Campbell and his son Donald set new speed records on land and water. The Campbells' vehicles were fitted with powerful engines that had originally been designed to power aircraft.

THE FIRST BLUE BIRD

Malcolm Campbell (1885–1948) broke the land speed record nine times between 1924 and 1935. He painted all of his racing cars blue and called them Blue Bird. Campbell set his first land speed record in the *Sunbeam 350HP Blue Bird*, reaching 146 miles (235 km) per hour on a course at Pendine Sands beach in Wales.

CAMPBELL-RAILTON BLUE BIRD

In 1935, Malcolm Campbell (right) broke the 300-mile (483 km) per hour barrier for the first time in his final record attempt. He was driving the *Campbell-Railton Blue Bird*, a purpose-built car designed by engineer Reid Railton. The car was fitted with a huge Rolls-Royce aircraft engine.

WATER SPEED RECORDS

Malcolm and Donald Campbell both set water speed records. Malcolm set his best time in 1939, reaching 142 miles (228 km) per hour on Coniston Water in the Lake District, England. Donald set the last of his seven new records in 1964, reaching 277 miles (445 km) per hour in his jet-powered *Bluebird K7* (left). Tragically, he was killed in a later attempt to break the record when he lost control of the boat.

LAST WHEEL-DRIVEN RECORD

Following his father's death in 1948, Donald Campbell (1921–1967) worked with Malcolm's chief engineer Leo Villa to make his own speed attempts. He set eight records on land and water in the 1950s and 1960s. He set a new land speed record in 1964 in the rocket-powered *Bluebird CN7*, which he took to a speed of 403 miles (649 km) per hour. This was the last time the record would be broken by a **wheel-driven car**.

JET CARS

In the 1950s, a number of new cars powered by jet engines were made. While they were too dangerous to take on the roads, jet cars were later developed to become the fastest cars of all, and every land speed record since 1964 has been set by a jet-powered car.

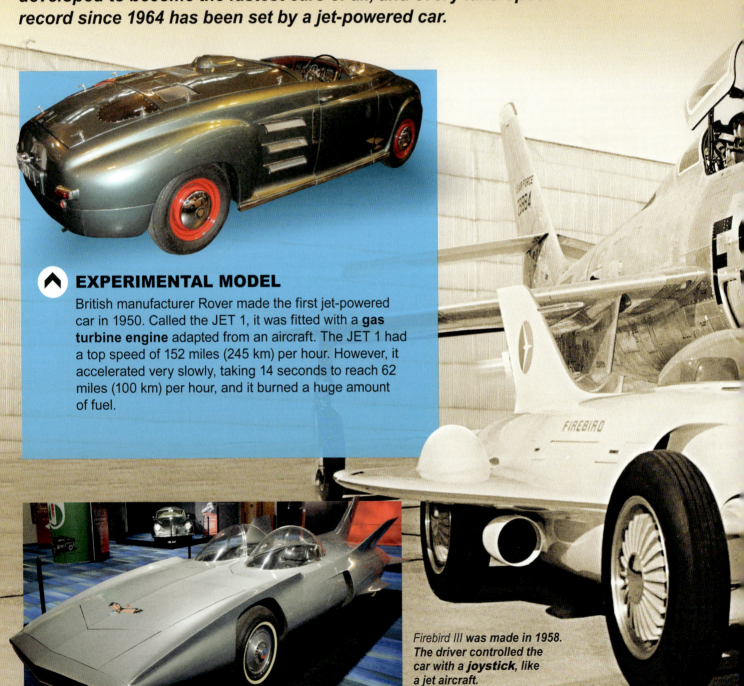

EXPERIMENTAL MODEL
British manufacturer Rover made the first jet-powered car in 1950. Called the JET 1, it was fitted with a **gas turbine engine** adapted from an aircraft. The JET 1 had a top speed of 152 miles (245 km) per hour. However, it accelerated very slowly, taking 14 seconds to reach 62 miles (100 km) per hour, and it burned a huge amount of fuel.

Firebird III was made in 1958. The driver controlled the car with a *joystick*, like a jet aircraft.

FIREBIRD

In 1953, US manufacturer General Motors produced the first of three jet-powered concept cars, *Firebird I*. It was shaped like a jet aircraft on wheels, with one seat in a bubble-topped cockpit. The designers hoped the car would reach 186 miles (300 km) per hour. It was taken to 99 miles (160 km) per hour in testing, but the driver had to slam on the brakes when the car started to take off!

JET POWER

The first jet cars used jet engines to turn their wheels. From 1963 onward, the most powerful record-breaking cars did not power the wheels. Instead, their jet engines moved the cars with a rapid jet of gas. These worked according to Newton's Third Law of Motion, which states that "Every action has an equal and opposite reaction." This means that the force of the gas moving out of the back of the car produces an equal and opposite force to push the car along.

Gases rush out.

Force pushes car in opposite direction.

JET KART

In 2018, Briton Colin Furze set the world record speed for a jet-powered go-kart. He drove his homemade kart to speeds of more than 62 miles (100 km) per hour.

SPEED IN THE
SIXTIES

In the 1960s, a race was on to produce the fastest jet-powered cars. Between 1963 and 1965, the land speed record was broken nine times at the Bonneville Salt Flats, as a group of American drivers spurred each other on. Over two years, they added more than 186 miles (300 km) per hour to the record.

First Spirit of America

SPIRIT OF AMERICA

Craig Breedlove (born 1937) drove a series of jet cars called Spirit of America, breaking the land speed record five times in the 1960s. He broke the record for the first time in the original *Spirit of America*. However, the FIA did not recognize his record at first because they classed his car as a motorcycle. In 1965, driving the four-wheeled *Spirit of America – Sonic 1*, Breedlove broke the 600-mile (965-km) per hour barrier for the first time.

Spirit of America – Sonic 1

BATTLE OF THE ROCKET CARS

October 13, 1964
Craig Breedlove
Spirit of America | 469 miles (754 km) per hour

October 27, 1964
Art Arfons
Green Monster | 537 miles (864 km) per hour

October 5, 1964
Art Arfons
Green Monster | 434 miles (699 km) per hour

October 15, 1964
Craig Breedlove
Spirit of America | 526 miles (847 km) per hour

GREEN MONSTER

Art Arfons (1926–2007) was Craig Breedlove's arch-rival. He broke the record three times in his *Green Monster* jet car, which he built with his brother Walt. Like Breedlove, Arfons powered his car with an engine from a military jet. His fastest speed was 577 miles (928 km) per hour, set in November 1965 and beaten by Breedlove a week later.

Cockpit of Green Monster

FASTEST WOMAN

In 1965, Craig Breedlove's wife, Lee (born 1937), made four separate runs in *Sonic 1* at Bonneville Salt Flats. She recorded a speed of 309 miles (496.5 km) per hour, making her the fastest woman in the world. Lee had been persuaded to drive the car by her husband in order to prevent a rival driver from attempting the record on that day. Her record stood until 2013, when it was beaten by fellow American Jessi Combs.

November 2, 1965
Craig Breedlove
Sonic 1 | 556 miles (894 km) per hour

November 7, 1965
Art Arfons
Green Monster | 577 miles (928 km) per hour

November 15, 1965
Craig Breedlove
Sonic 1 | 601 miles (967 km) per hour

PIONEERING WOMEN

In the early years of cars, women were often discouraged from driving on the road and refused entry into races. Over the years, a number of determined female drivers have defied expectations to forge driving careers that inspired many other women to take the wheel.

> ### CHAMPIONING WOMEN'S RIGHTS

In the face of widespread opposition to female drivers, British motorist Dorothy Levitt (1882–1922) competed in races between 1903 and 1908. She set the women's land speed record of 91 miles (146 km) per hour in 1906. Levitt toured the country giving lectures encouraging women to take up motoring.

In a book on motoring for women published in 1909, Levitt advised female drivers to always to carry a hand mirror, and to use it occasionally to see what was behind them. In this way, she helped to invent the **rearview mirror**, which was first fitted to road cars seven years later!

The 1911 Marmon Wasp was the first racing car to be fitted with a rearview mirror.

GRAND PRIX DRIVER
French driver Hellé Nice (1900–1984) first competed in all-women races in 1929, proving her talent by taking the women's world speed record. From 1931, she drove against men in Grand Prix races around the world. In 1936, Nice survived a terrifying crash in the São Paulo Grand Prix in Brazil. The crash killed six other people and left Nice in a coma for three days after she was thrown from her car. She made a comeback to racing the following year.

DANICA PATRICK
American Danica Patrick (born 1982) is the only woman to have won an **IndyCar** Series race, taking the winning flag at the 2008 Indy Japan 300. Patrick completed the 304-mile (489-km) race around the speedy oval track with an average speed of 164 miles (264 km) per hour.

Danica Patrick competing at the 2011 IndyCar Series Toyota Grand Prix at Long Beach, California, USA.

BREAKING THE SOUND BARRIER

The current land speed record of 763 miles (1,228 km) per hour was set in 1997 by the jet car **Thrust Super Sonic Car**, or **Thrust SSC**, over a course in Black Rock Desert, Nevada, USA. This was the first time a car had ever exceeded the **speed of sound**, a feat that has never yet been repeated.

Fighter pilot Andy Green

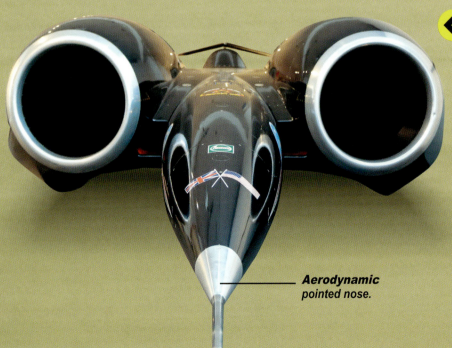

ROCKET ON WHEELS

The huge car was 54 feet (16.5 m) long and 12 feet (3.7 m) wide, and weighed more than 11 tons (10 tonnes). It was powered by two Rolls-Royce Spey **turbofan engines**, developed for fighter jets, which burned 4.7 gallons (18 l) of fuel per second. The car was driven by fighter pilot Andy Green, a wing commander in the Royal Air Force.

Aerodynamic pointed nose.

TURBOFAN

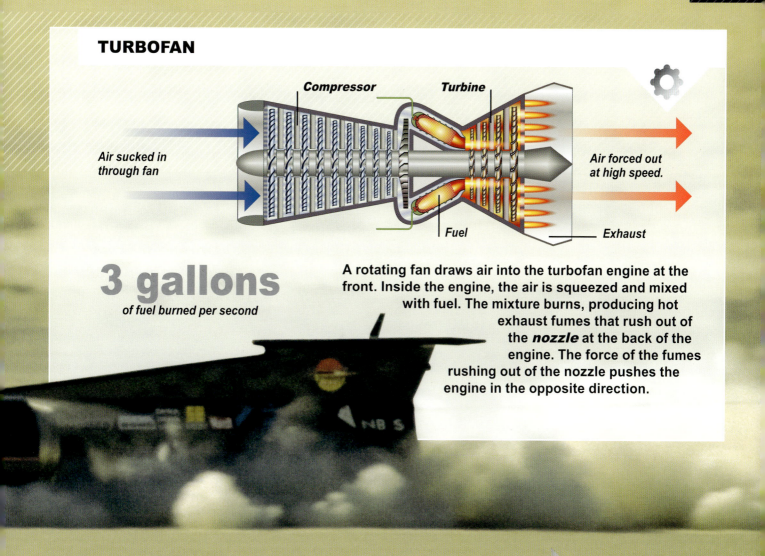

Compressor | Turbine
Air sucked in through fan
Air forced out at high speed.
Fuel | Exhaust

3 gallons
of fuel burned per second

A rotating fan draws air into the turbofan engine at the front. Inside the engine, the air is squeezed and mixed with fuel. The mixture burns, producing hot exhaust fumes that rush out of the *nozzle* at the back of the engine. The force of the fumes rushing out of the nozzle pushes the engine in the opposite direction.

Thrust SSC *produced maximum power of*

100,600 hp
That's 500 times more powerful than an average family car.

> ### RICHARD NOBLE
Thrust SSC was the brainchild of British businessman Richard Noble (born 1946). He already held the land speed record with his previous car *Thrust 2*, which Noble himself had driven to a speed of 633 miles (1,019 km) per hour in 1983. *Thrust 2* had been powered by a single jet engine. Noble designed *Thrust SSC* with two jet engines to give it greater power.

Single jet engine at the back of the car.

SPEED IN THE FUTURE

Now that the speed of sound has been broken, the race is on to make the first car to break the 1,000 mph (1,609 km/h) barrier. These are the projects that aim to be the first to make it.

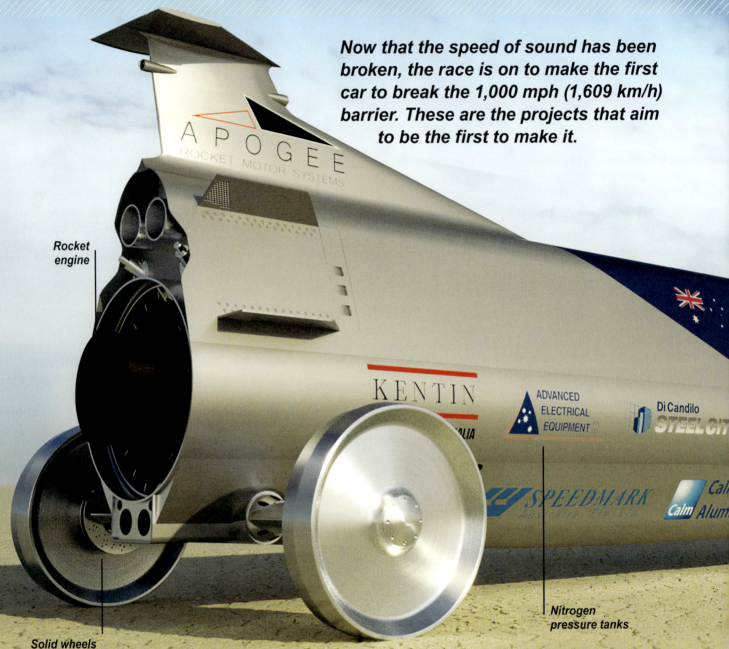

Rocket engine

Solid wheels

Nitrogen pressure tanks

AUSSIE INVADER 5R

Aussie Invader 5R is powered by a single huge rocket, which produces 200,000 **horsepower**. That's twice as powerful as *Thrust SSC*. The Australian team that have built it hope to reach 1,000 mph in 20 seconds, and to maintain this speed for five seconds.

Aussie Invader 5R aims to accelerate to 1,000 mph in just

20 seconds!

 ## BURNING FUEL

Aussie Invader 5R's rocket works using two kinds of liquid fuel. When the two are mixed, they burn. The car will create huge power by forcing the fuel together under high pressure. This will cause the fuel to burn very quickly, giving about 25 seconds of extreme power, burning over 3.3 tons (3 tonnes) of fuel in the process.

 ## BLOODHOUND LSR

Since 2008, the team that built *Thrust SSC* has been developing a new car. Named *Bloodhound LSR* (which stands for Land Speed Record), the car will be driven once again by British pilot Andy Green. He took it to over 621 miles (1,000 km) per hour in tests in 2019. *Bloodhound LSR* is powered by a pair of rockets and an electric motor.

Cockpit

Nose cone

 ## BULLET PROJECT

While both *Aussie Invader 5R* and *Bloodhound LSR* are enormous machines, the Australian Bullet Project is designing a much smaller and lighter car to break the 1,000 mph barrier. The *RV1* is a rocket car that weighs 3.3 tons (3 tonnes) – less than one third of the weight of *Aussie Invader 5R*. Its designers hope that its light weight will allow it to accelerate very quickly.

TOP FUEL DRAGSTERS

Top Fuel dragsters are the cars with the greatest acceleration in the world, reaching speeds in excess of 311 miles (500 km) per hour in just a couple of seconds. They race one another side-by-side over straight 1,001-foot (305-m) courses, and the whole race is over in under five seconds.

Before a race, the cars perform a burnout to get their wheels up to full racing temperature by spinning the wheels on the spot.

The NHRA Arizona Nationals is held at the Wild Horse Pass Motorsports Park, Chandler, a track that is famed for its super-fast racing conditions.

G-FORCES

The extreme acceleration of Top Fuel dragsters puts the driver's body under enormous strain. At peak acceleration, the drivers are pinned to the backs of their seat by a force that is up to eight times the strength of **gravity**, or 8 g. This makes them feel as if they were eight times heavier than they are. The forces are similar to those experienced by astronauts when rockets launch into space.

 ## EXPLOSIVE FUEL

Top Fuel dragsters use a special fuel called nitromethane to maximize their performance. This highly explosive substance burns very quickly without the need to inject high volumes of air into the engine. The results are dramatic. Any unburned fuel in the exhaust causes flames when it mixes with the air. The burning fuel is also incredibly loud – at up to 150 **decibels**, it is louder than a rock concert and spectators are advised to wear earplugs during races to protect their hearing.

 ## RECORD RUN

Top Fuel records are recorded by the National Hot Rod Association (NHRA) at official Top Fuel events. At the NHRA's Arizona Nationals event in 2018, American Tony Schumacher recorded the fastest run ever when he completed the course in 3.649 seconds. He reached a maximum speed of 335 miles (539 km) per hour.

 ## DRAGSTER PIONEER

American driver and engineer Don Garlits (born 1932) set many of the early speed records in Top Fuel drag racing. He also introduced many safety features. Following an accident in 1970, in which Garlits lost part of his foot, he redesigned his car to place the engine behind the driver. Today, all dragsters follow this design. He was still racing well into his 80s, and in 2014, he recorded a speed of 184 miles (296 km) per hour in an all-electric drag car.

TRACK RACING
FORMULA 1

Formula 1 (F1) is the fastest, most prestigious track racing series in the world, and cars reach up to 217 miles (350 km) per hour during races. The cars not only need to be fast in a straight line, they also need to be able to take tight corners at high speed. Each year, teams produce a new car, which must meet strict rules regarding size, weight, and fuel economy.

The large front and rear wings produce *downforce* when air passes over them. This helps to keep the car on the road when it is taking corners at high speed.

⌃ EARLY F1 CARS
Today's F1 cars are fitted with safety features to protect drivers in the event of a crash. When the competition started in the 1950s, drivers were almost entirely unprotected, and fatal crashes were common. However, the early tube-shaped cars were very fast in a straight line. For instance, the Maserati 250F (above) had a top speed of 180 miles (290 km) per hour – almost as fast as modern F1 cars. Lacking the aerodynamics of modern cars, however, it was much slower around corners.

⌃ CHAMPION CAR
Since 2014, the Mercedes-AMG Petronas team has dominated F1. Mercedes' winning car for 2019, the W10 EQ Power+, was powered by a 1.6-liter engine and two electric motors.

23

Gearbox neutral

Shift paddle left

Shift paddle right

Radio

⌃ HIGH TECH CONTROLS

F1 cars are packed with the latest technology. The drivers can operate the controls without ever letting go of the steering wheel.

❯ FORMULA E

Today's F1 cars are hybrids, meaning that they are powered by a combination of a gas engine and electric motors. In the future, F1 may become all-electric. Since 2014, electric cars have raced in a series called Formula E. All drivers drive the same Spark SRT05e cars, which have a top speed of 174 miles (280 km) per hour.

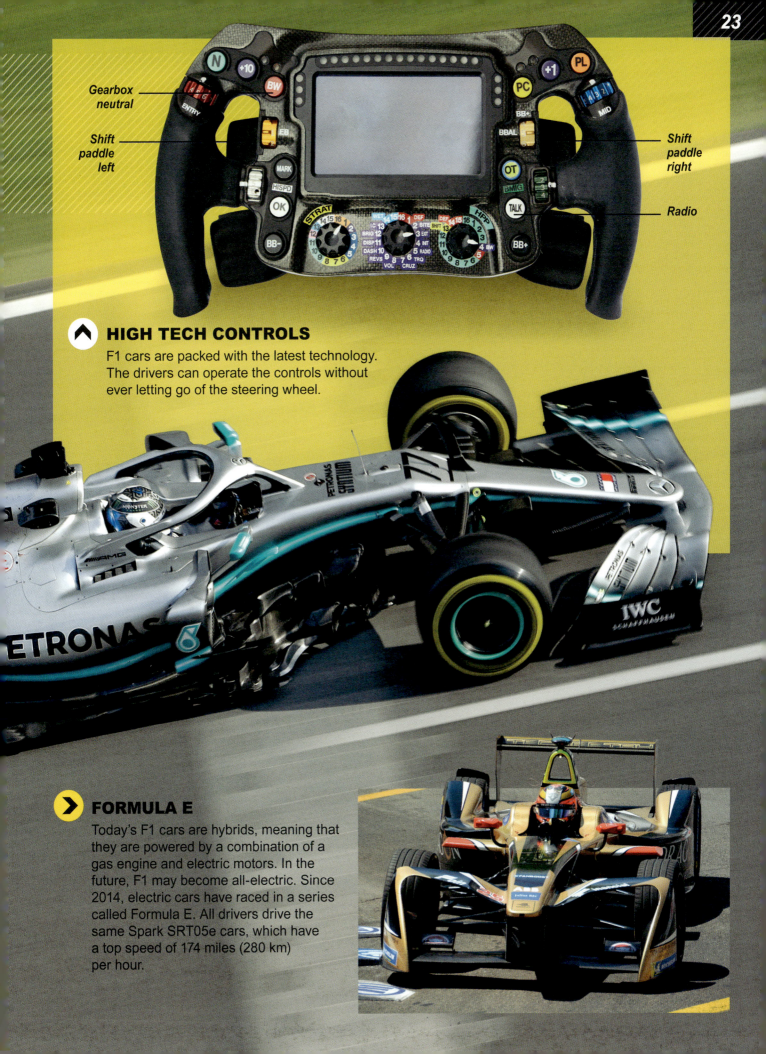

SPEED AND ENDURANCE

During endurance races, cars drive as far as they can in a set period of time. The World Endurance Championship is a series of races held over time periods ranging from six hours to 24 hours. The fastest cars in the races are known as Le Mans Prototypes, or LMPs.

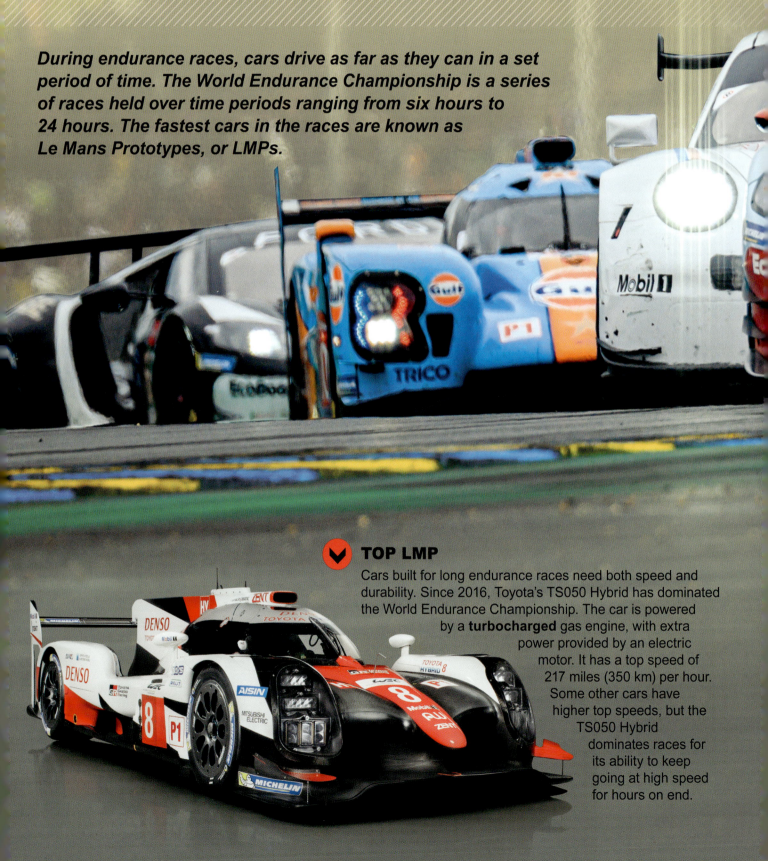

TOP LMP

Cars built for long endurance races need both speed and durability. Since 2016, Toyota's TS050 Hybrid has dominated the World Endurance Championship. The car is powered by a **turbocharged** gas engine, with extra power provided by an electric motor. It has a top speed of 217 miles (350 km) per hour. Some other cars have higher top speeds, but the TS050 Hybrid dominates races for its ability to keep going at high speed for hours on end.

24 HOURS OF LE MANS

The oldest and most prestigious endurance race in the world is the 24 hours of Le Mans in France. The race is held around the *Circuit de la Sarthe*, a 8.4-mile-long (13.6-km) circuit that mixes purpose-built track with sections of public roads. Teams of drivers take turns to race non-stop for a full day and night.

> FULL THROTTLE

The *Circuit de la Sarthe* is a very fast track and the drivers spend 85 percent of their time at full power. The fastest section of the track is the 4-mile (6-km) Mulsanne Straight, where cars reach their maximum speed. By the 1980s, LMPs were reaching speeds of more than 249 miles (400 km) along the Mulsanne Straight. Following two fatal accidents, two chicanes (bends) were added to slow the cars down. The record distance for the modern circuit was set in 2018. The winning Toyota TS050 Hybrid covered 3,285 miles (5,287 km), almost the distance from London to New York, at an average speed of 137 miles (220 km) per hour.

The cars drive through the night. Nighttime racing is particularly dangerous and drivers need to remain fully alert.

FASTEST CARS
ON THE ROAD

The fastest road-legal cars are called supercars. These limited-edition sports cars are built using technology developed for racing cars. Their owners need to take them to the racetrack if they want to test out their cars' full power!

▼ AGERA RS

In 2020, the fastest road car in the world was the Koenigsegg Agera RS, with a maximum straight-line speed of 285 miles (458 km) per hour. One of the keys to the car's high performance is its aerodynamic shape. It allows air to pass smoothly around and through it while producing just the right amount of downforce to keep the car safely on the road.

This computer image shows the air flow around and through the car.

FASTEST ROAD CAR

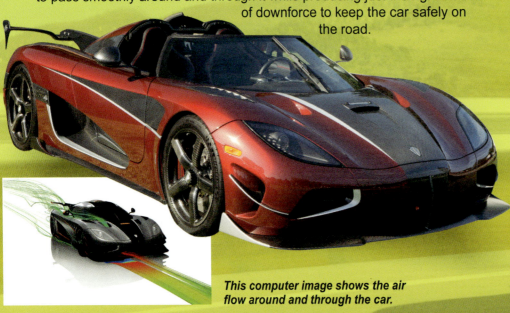

1986
Porsche 959 | 198 miles (319 km) per hour

1969
Lamborghini Miura | 171 miles (275 km) per hour

1993
McLaren F1 | 221 miles (355 km) per hour

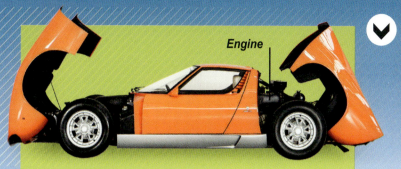
Engine

FIRST SUPERCAR
The Lamborghini Miura was the first supercar. It was the fastest road-legal car when it was produced in 1967, with a top speed of 171 miles (275 km) per hour. As in an F1 car, the engine was positioned behind the driver to give the car perfect balance. This design has become standard for all supercars.

GOING ELECTRIC
The earliest racing cars were electric, and the supercars of the future will also be electric as the world moves away from gasoline. The fastest electric road car in 2020 was the Rimac C-2. It has a maximum speed of 25 miles (415 km) per hour and can accelerate from 0–62 miles (100 km) in just 1.9 seconds – the same as an F1 car!

BUGATTI VEYRON
In 2005, the Bugatti Veyron was the first road-legal car to pass 249 miles (400 km), recording a top speed of 254 miles (408 km) per hour. A special super-powerful edition of the Veyron, the 16.4 Super Sport, reached 268 miles (431 km) per hour in 2010. It held the record until 2017, when it was beaten by the Koenigsegg Agera RS.

2010
Bugatti Veyron 16.4 Super Sport | 268 miles (431 km) per hour

2017
Koenigsegg Agera RS | 278 miles (447 km) per hour

POWERED BY THE SUN

Every two years, teams race one another across Australia in cars powered solely by the sun, at an event called the World Solar Challenge. Starting in Darwin in the north, the drivers finish more than 1,864 miles (3,000 km) away in Adelaide in the south. These cars develop technology that could one day be used to power clean, efficient cars on the road.

› POWER IN THE DAYTIME

Solar panels on the cars use energy from the sun to generate electricity. The solar cars use the electricity to power motors, which turn the wheels. One of the challenges for solar cars is that they cannot operate in the dark! The cars in the World Solar Challenge stop each night and start again the following morning. In the future, to keep moving at night, solar cars will need to charge a battery during the day. The manufacturers of electric cars are currently looking for new ways to make lighter and more efficient batteries.

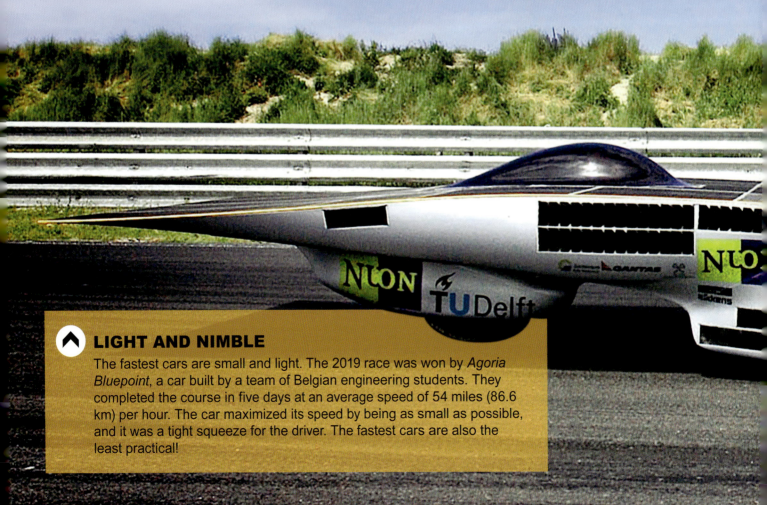

⌃ LIGHT AND NIMBLE

The fastest cars are small and light. The 2019 race was won by *Agoria Bluepoint*, a car built by a team of Belgian engineering students. They completed the course in five days at an average speed of 54 miles (86.6 km) per hour. The car maximized its speed by being as small as possible, and it was a tight squeeze for the driver. The fastest cars are also the least practical!

CRUISER CLASS

In addition to a class for ultra-lightweight single-seaters, the race includes a class for two- or four-seater cruisers. Competitors are judged not only for their speed but also for their practicality. Dutch team Solar Team Eindhoven won the Cruiser class every year from 2013 to 2019. In 2019, they won with their four-seater *Stella Era* (left). In addition to power from the solar panels, the car also powered motors by recovering energy from its brakes, making it even more efficient.

SOLAR SPEED RECORD

The world speed record for solar-powered cars was set in 2014 by a team of Australian students with their car *Sunswift eVe*. It completed a 311-mile (500-km) course at an average speed of 66 miles (107 km) per hour. In 2016, it became Australia's first-ever road-legal solar car.

GLOSSARY

aerodynamics
The way in which a gas or liquid moves around a solid object as it passes through. Cars are designed with an aerodynamic shape that allows air to move around them smoothly.

compressor
A machine inside a gas turbine engine that increases the pressure of the gas.

decibel
A unit of measurement for the loudness of sounds.

downforce
A force that pushes down on an object when it moves through the air. At high speeds, cars need to produce downforce to stop them from taking off from the ground.

gas turbine engine
An engine that burns fuel to drive a turbine.

gravity
A force of attraction between objects. Earth's gravity pulls objects toward the center of Earth and gives us our weight.

horsepower
A unit of measurement for power, or the rate at which work is done. One horsepower is roughly equal to the power of one strong horse.

IndyCar
The top division of open-wheel car racing in North America.

joystick
A stick that can be moved to different angles, often used to control aircraft.

nozzle
A device that controls the rate at which air or liquid comes out of a tube.

rearview mirror
A mirror positioned next to the driver in a car to see traffic behind them.

rocket-powered car
A car that is powered forward by a stream of fast-moving air that shoots out of a rocket at the rear.

solar panels
Sets of cells that convert the energy of the sun into electricity.

speed of sound
The speed at which sound travels through the air. At sea level, the speed of sound is approximately 771 miles (1,240 km) per hour.

turbine
A machine with blades that spin when a gas or liquid is passed through them.

turbocharged
Refers to an engine that is given extra power by a turbo. The turbo uses energy from the exhaust to force extra air into the engine, allowing the fuel to burn more efficiently.

turbofan engine
A kind of jet engine that sucks air in at the front using a fan.

wheel-driven car
A car whose engine is attached to some or all of the wheels.

SPEED FILE

FASTEST JET CAR
Thrust SSC
Max speed
763 miles (1,228 km) per hour
Set: 1997

FASTEST WHEEL-DRIVEN CAR
Turbinator II
Max speed
503 miles (810 km) per hour
Set: 2018

FASTEST GAS-ENGINE CAR
Railton Mobil Special
Max speed
394 miles (634 km) per hour
Set: 1947

FASTEST ELECTRIC CAR
Venturi VBB-3
Max speed
341 miles (549 km) per hour
Set: 2016

FASTEST SPEED IN A TOP FUEL DRAG RACE
Tony Schumacher
Max speed
336 miles (541 km) per hour
Set: 2018

FASTEST ROAD-LEGAL CAR
Koenigsegg Agera RS
Max speed
278 miles (447 km) per hour
Set: 2017

FASTEST STEAM-POWERED CAR
British Steam Car Inspiration
Max speed
139 miles (225 km) per hour
Set: 2009

FASTEST SOLAR-POWERED CAR
Sunswift eVe
Max speed
66 miles (107 km) per hour, average over 311 miles (500 km).
Set: 2014

INDEX

24 Hours of Le Mans 25

Agera RS 26
Agoria Bluepoint 28
Arfons, Art 13
Aussie Invader 5R 18

Babs 7
Black Rock Desert 16
Bloodhound LSR 19
Blue Bird cars 8–9
Bluebird CN7 9
Bluebird K7 9
Bonneville Salt Flats 6, 12–13
Breedlove, Craig 12–13
Breedlove, Lee 13
Bugatti Veyron 27
Bullet Project 19

Campbell, Donald 8–9
Campbell, Malcolm 8–9
Campbell-Railton Blue Bird 8
Chasseloup-Laubat, Gaston 4
Circuit de la Sarthe 25
Combs, Jesse 13
Coniston Water 9

Easter Egg 5
electric cars 4, 23, 27, 28–29

FIA (International Federation of Automobiles) 6–7, 12
Firebird I 11
Firebird III 10
Formula E 23
Furze, Colin 11

Garlits, Don 21
General Motors 11
g-forces 21
Green, Andy 16, 19

hybrids 23, 24

IndyCar 15

Jeantaud car 4
Jenatzy, Camille 4
JET 1 10
jet kart 11

Koenigsegg 26

Lamborghini 27
Le Mans Prototype (LMP) 24–25
Levitt, Dorothy 14

Marmon Wasp 14
Marriott, Fred 5
Maserati 250F 22
Mercedes-AMG Petronas 22
Miura 27
Mulsanne Straight 25

Newton's Third Law of Motion 11
NHRA Arizona Nationals 20–21
Nice, Hellé 15
Noble, Richard 17

Opel-Rak 5

Parry-Thomas, JG 7
Patrick, Danica 15
Pendine Sands 7, 8

Railton, Reid 8
Rimac C-2 27
rocket cars 5, 9
Rolls-Royce 8, 16
Rover 10
RV1 19

Schumacher, Tony 21
Serpollet, Leon 5
solar power 28–29
sound, speed of 16
Spark SRT05e 23
Speed Week (Bonneville) 6
Spirit of America 12
Spirit of America – Sonic 1 12
Stanley Steamer 5
steam cars 5
Stella Era 29
Sunbeam 350HP Blue Bird 8
Sunswift eVe 29

Thrust 2 17
Thrust SSC 16–17, 18
Top Fuel 21
Toyota 24
TS050 Hybrid 24, 25
turbofan engine 16, 17

Villa, Leo 9
von Opel, Fritz 5

water speed record 9
World Endurance Championship 24–25
World Solar Challenge 28–29